ABANDONED GARY, INDIANA

CITY OF THE CENTURY

DAVID BULIT

America Through Time is an imprint of Fonthill Media LLC
www.through-time.com
office@through-time.com

Published by Arcadia Publishing by arrangement with Fonthill Media LLC
For all general information, please contact Arcadia Publishing:
Telephone: 843-853-2070
Fax: 843-853-0044
E-mail: sales@arcadiapublishing.com
For customer service and orders:
Toll-Free 1-888-313-2665

www.arcadiapublishing.com

First published 2022

ISBN 978-1-63499-407-1

Typeset in Trade Gothic 10pt on 15pt
Printed and bound in England

CONTENTS

ABOUT THE AUTHOR

DAVID BULIT is a photographer, author, and historian from Miami, Florida. He has published a number of books on abandoned and forgotten locales throughout the United States and continues to advocate for preserving these historic landmarks. His work has been featured throughout the world in news outlets such as the *Miami New Times*, the *Florida Times-Union*, the *Orlando Sentinel*, NPR, Yahoo News, MSN, the *Daily Mail*, *The Sun*, and many others. You can find more of his work at davidbulit.com as well as amazon.com/author/davidbulit.

INTRODUCTION

Gary, Indiana, was founded in 1906 by the United States Steel Corporation as the home of its new plant, Gary Works, the largest steel mill in the world at the time of its construction. It was named after Judge Elbert Henry Gary, who was the founding chairman of the U.S. Steel Corporation. Gary's formative years saw an influx of immigrants, primarily from eastern European countries, many of whom found their calling at the steel mill. By 1920, nearly 30% of the city's population was foreign-born and a further 30% had at least one foreign-born parent. Many notable people were born in this once great city, such as Michael Jackson, Janet Jackson, and countless sports athletes from boxing to basketball.

The city has a long and storied history of civil unrest since its founding, be it the Steel Strike of 1919 or the civil rights movement of the 1950s and 60s. This unrest eventually led to the election of Mayor Richard G. Hatcher in 1967, one of the nation's first black mayors, and the "white flight" that followed suit. This event—followed by the gradual decline of the steel mill, which simply could not compete with overseas competition—marked the beginning of the city's downward spiral. In the late 1990s and early 2000s, Gary had the highest percentage of African Americans of U.S. cities with a population of 100,000 or more. This no longer applies, as Gary's population has fallen far below 100,000. The city was once regarded as "Little Chicago, a playground of sorts for such great architects as Frank Lloyd Wright, George W. Maher, and William Holabird. The Gary Department of Redevelopment has estimated that one-third of all homes and buildings in the city are unoccupied and/or abandoned. Today, the once great city is a ghost town considered by many as "The Most Miserable City" in America.

1

CITY METHODIST CHURCH

Since the city of Gary's founding in 1906, there has always been a Methodist church within the city. In 1916, Dr. William Seaman became its pastor, a man with a dream of a new church to serve the burgeoning city. He wanted a religious presence in the neighborhood which was dotted with numerous brothels and taverns. With the financial assistance from U.S. Steel, the chief employer of the city, what would later be known as City Methodist Church was erected in 1926 on land donated by the steel company. Designed by the Lowe & Bollenbacher architectural firm of Chicago, the sanctuary was just part of a large nine-story complex which included an adjoining theater called Seaman Hall, which could seat 1,000 people, and contained corporate offices, a gymnasium, a Sunday School, and a dining hall. Judge Elbert Gary, chairman of U.S. Steel and who the city was named after, personally donated an ornate, four-manual Skinner organ. The church held its first service on October 3, 1926, and by 1927, it had a congregation of 1,700 with a staff of six, including an assistant minister, directors of athletics and Christian education, a music master, and a secretary.

Since its opening, William Seaman had an ever-growing group of detractors who complained about the building's Roman Catholic overtones and that it was merely a monument to himself. Immediately after opening, this group began labeling the building "Seaman's folly." Despite its beauty, the building was constructed at a great cost and stature for a congregation and city of that size. Maintenance costs would be a financial burden on the church throughout its lifetime, eventually becoming one of its downfalls.

To some degree, the church navigated race relations in a polarized city, opening its doors to civic, social, and spiritual gatherings. Seaman was fairly successful in promoting the community hall as a religiously neutral ground for artistic and civic events, welcoming Latinos and Eastern Europeans. Although Black residents were not allowed to worship there, they were still allowed to utilize the church's amenities. By 1929, Seaman grew unpopular among his parishioners due to his views and methods and was involuntarily transferred to an Ohio church. Ironically, Seaman's successor was so unpopular, the congregation wished for Seaman to return. William Seaman died in an automobile accident in 1944, his body was cremated and returned to Gary to be interred in the City Methodist Church's sanctuary, as per his wishes. The church would fail to broaden its white middle-class consistency, leading to its eventual demise.

Gary rapidly declined in the 1960s and 1970s, and the church likewise. As stated previously, the congregation consisted of mostly white middle-class members, many of which were lost due to white flight as crime rates in the city soared and Gary's social makeup changed. By 1973, membership had fallen to 320, about a third of whom regularly attended. Offerings weren't enough to pay the utility bills, let alone the numerous repairs needed on the aging structure. After attempts to sell the building to another congregation proved fruitless due to the expense needed on maintaining the building, the decision was eventually made to close the City Methodist Church on October 5, 1975.

In 1994, City Methodist Church was added to the National Register of Historic Places as a contributing structure of the Gary City Center Historic District. Over the years, the church slowly degraded with attempts to renovate it, but none came to fruition before the Great Gary Arson of 1997.

On the night of October 12, 1997, a fire started on the second floor of the abandoned Goldblatt's Department Store just north of the Broadway Shopping Mall and quickly spread, engulfing the Memorial Auditorium to the east and the Radigan building to the north, then across to the roofs of the Genesis Towers building and City Methodist Church. Most of the buildings damaged were abandoned before the fire, and so they were quickly demolished. The fire dealt a considerable amount of damage to City Methodist Church, collapsing most of the roof and accelerating the building's deterioration. In 2011, a portion of the roof above the sanctuary caved in and thieves have removed most of the interior fixtures. After decades of abandonment, the church remains a symbol of urban blight and a beacon to photographers and explorers around the country.

To the right of the church, one can see the small historic marker which was installed only in recent years.

Above: The church was designed by Lowe & Bollenbacher, who also designed the First Christian Church in Bloomington, IN.

Left: This entryway into the church has caved in since the church's abandonment.

Right: This was one of the many fireplaces throughout the building.

Below: Although this angle of the church has been photographed countless times, it is actually looking towards the back of the church.

Above: Up above, the green tarp was installed to hold up debris falling off the bell tower but has since ripped.

Left: Small pieces of stained glass are still present, although the bulk of it has been destroyed by vandals.

The cremains of William Seaman are buried within this sanctuary.

A lobby located between the church's sanctuary and auditorium.

Above left: Old trim can still be seen on the ceilings.

Above right: This portion of the lobby has caved in.

A lecturing room on the ground floor of the building.

Above: The church's parish hall was later called Seaman's Hall in his honor.

Right: "666" and a pentagram are spray painted on a door, most likely by edgy teenagers.

Above: A small classroom which was later used by the local university.

Left: What's left of a fireplace in one of the classrooms.

A small storage area.

This area of the building was used by the local university into the 90s.

2

PALACE THEATER

The Palace Theater was designed by renowned theater architect John Eberson in the atmospheric style; the auditorium ceiling was painted blue to give the illusion of an open sky and decorative elements were added to give visitors the illusion of being in a distant land. Built by Maximillian Dubois, construction on the theater began in 1924 and it was open the following year. From the time of its opening, the Palace was one of the grandest venues in the city featuring live stage shows, vaudeville acts, and motion pictures.

When the U.S. Steel plant went into decline, so did the rest of Gary, including the Palace Theater. In 1968, 10th grader Aldrid Black was stabbed to death in the theater lobby after a showing of Bonnie and Clyde. Violent incidents continued until 1972 when a young lady was attacked in the women's restroom and the Palace Theater was closed immediately after. It reopened three years later as the Star Palace Theater but closed down after the owner was unable to pay the heating or water bills. With the help of a government grant, the theater reopened a final time in 1976 as the Star Academy of Performing Arts and Sciences but was shuttered after funds from the grant ran out. In 1987, private investors attempted to rehabilitate the area with plans to renovate the theater and other nearby storefronts. Unfortunately, the plan was scrapped after the opening of the first restaurant proved unsuccessful.

When the Miss USA pageant was held in Gary in 2002, Donald Trump renovated the front of the theater with sheets of plywood. The plywood covering the windows was painted to depict a false interior and an external marquee was mounted along the front which read "Jackson Five Tonite," although the Jackson Five never performed at the Palace. After Michael Jackson's death in 2009, plastic signs reading "Jackson Five Forever" were added to both sides of the marquee, but they have since been lost to the wind. In 1994, it was added to the National Register of Historic Places as a contributing structure of the Gary City Center Historic District.

The facade was decorated for the Miss USA pageant held in Gary in 2002.

Though it sits on Gary's main street, the area is extremely desolate.

The Palace was designed by architect John Eberson, best known for the development and promotion of movie palace designs in the atmospheric theatre style.

Looking at what would have been the entryways into the auditorium.

The lobby area of the theater.

3

H. GORDON & SONS DEPARTMENT STORE

The former H. Gordon and Sons Department Store is an abandoned four-story brick building located in downtown Gary, Indiana. The building was originally constructed for the Benevolent and Protective Order of Elks to serve as a lodge. In 1923, architecture firm George W. Maher & Son was commissioned to design a new temple of the Order as they had outgrown their original location on West 6th Avenue and Washington Street. The building was designed in the Prairie School style with the first floor containing commercial storefronts while the upper floors contained lodge rooms, offices, bars, and banquet halls.

The Benevolent and Protective Order of Elks moved out of the building in 1934, which was then remodeled for H. Gordon and Sons department store. On July 14, 1939, H. Gordon and Sons announced that it would close its store in nearby Whiting and consolidate it with its downtown Gary location. As part of the consolidation, a $75,000 renovation was planned for its Gary location involving the addition of a fourth floor, and new departments throughout the store.

In September 1971, the Lake County Welfare Department signed a lease agreement to relocate from the county courthouse to the H. Gordon and Sons department store building. H. Gordon and Sons planned to continue operating at the location until January 1, 1973, but just a year later, in September 1972, it was announced that H. Gordon and Sons was closing due to the declining downtown area and a lack of sales.

In January 1973, the food stamp offices moved into the main floor and basement of the H. Gordon and Sons building and the county welfare department followed by moving into the second, third, and fourth floors. In the early 1990s, the welfare department, renamed Division of Family and Children, began looking for larger offices due to a lack of space for its computers. The adjoining Sears, Roebuck & Company building, abandoned in 1974, was chosen and in early 1993, work began on a $6 million renovation of the new site with construction estimated to be completed by July 1993. The project was delayed by over a year due to supplier and financial issues and was completed in late 1995. Shortly after, the Division of Family and Children move out of the former H. Gordon and Sons building into its new location

In 1994, it was added to the National Register of Historic Places as a contributing structure of the Gary City Center Historic District. Since its vacancy, the building's interior wooden framework is beyond repair as large portions of the floors have collapsed due to water damage throughout the entire building.

An escalator in the ruined H. Gordon & Sons department store.

The second floor of the building.

Decaying display cases, although it is unknown what department this was.

A check dated March 23, 1959, for the amount of $34.15.

4

MEMORIAL AUDITORIUM

The Gary Memorial Auditorium is an abandoned civic center in Gary, Indiana, constructed to commemorate residents of the city of Gary that were killed fighting in World War I. Commissioned by the Gary Land Company, a subsidiary of the U.S. Steel Company, the building was designed by local architect Joseph Henry Wildermuth, who had previously worked for the Gary School Board designing new school buildings.

Construction on the Memorial Auditorium was completed in 1927 at the cost of $5 million, featuring a gymnasium and auditorium with a seating capacity of 5,000. The auditorium's stage was the largest in the region at the time of its construction and the asbestos curtain was the largest of its kind. The building's function was influenced by Gary's first school superintendent William Wirt, whose Work-Study-Play system of education drew international praise. The auditorium's floor seats were removable, allowing the building to be used as an art center, host school graduations, basketball games, music concerts, and boxing matches. Some notable events include the annual Golden Gloves Boxing Tournaments between 1939 and 1959, a performance by Frank Sinatra in 1945 in an attempt to ease tensions as schools attempted to desegregate, a campaign speech by President Harry Truman, and a city-wide talent contest held in the 1960s, which the Jackson Five won first place in.

The Memorial Auditorium closed in 1972 as the city was declining. There were plans to reopen the building as a Sports Hall of Fame, a museum exhibit for local history, and a performing arts center, but the plans were scrapped after the Great Gary Arson of 1997, the same fire that severely damaged the City Methodist Church. By the end, eight buildings were either severely damaged or completely destroyed, and only one-fourth of the Memorial Auditorium remained.

In 1994, it was added to the National Register of Historic Places as a contributing structure of the Gary City Center Historic District. Unfortunately, it was reported in 2019 that the building would be razed to be replaced with a thirty-eight-unit housing project for seniors and middle-income residents, but it wasn't until August 25, 2020, that demolition of the structure began.

The top of the structure reads "ART."

Across the front of it reads "GARY PUBLIC SCHOOLS MEMORIAL AUDITORIUM."

The corner of the building here reads "MUSIC."

Inside what remains of the auditorium. The main portion of the building was destroyed in a fire in 1997.

This portion of the structure had multiple floors, although only two were accessible at the time of my visit.

5

UNITED STATES POST OFFICE

The former United States Post Office located in downtown Gary, Indiana was constructed in 1936 as part of the New Deal, a series of programs, public works projects, financial reforms, and regulations established by President Franklin D. Roosevelt to respond to needs for relief, reform, and recovery from the Great Depression. The new post office replaced the two-story brick building known as the Gary Building, also known as the Post Office Block, once located on the corner of Fifth and Broadway.

The Art Moderne style structure was designed by Howard Lovewell Cheney who worked for the Public Buildings Branch of the U.S. Treasury Department from 1934 to 1942. His portfolio consists mostly of federal buildings due to his time working for the government, many of which are listed on the National Register of Historic Places including the Miami Beach Post Office, the United States Post Office and Courthouse in Peoria, Illinois, and the original Washington National Airport building. The building features smooth stuccoed walls reaching three stories in height set upon a black granite base with the only decorative embellishments being a relief of an American Eagle over the main entry. A virtually identical post office can be found in Marion, Indiana.

Although many sources claim this post office branch was closed in the 1970s, around the time the city was on the decline, there are no records indicating when it did close. In 1994, it was added to the National Register of Historic Places as a contributing structure of the Gary City Center Historic District.

The building was designed by Howard Lovewell Cheney who worked for the Public Buildings Branch of the U.S. Treasury Department.

The front lobby of the post office.

Another angle of the front lobby.

Moss growing in what was the sorting area.

Above: The floor of the sorting area was made of wood blocks, which can be seen here.

Right: Inside an office adjacent to the sorting area.

Back view of the USPS clerk windows.

The skylights have allowed for extensive water damage throughout the building.

Right: A staircase leading up into the offices.

Below: This area led outside to the back bay area for delivery trucks.

Above: Up on the second floor of the building.

Left: Looking down a hallway on the second floor.

Right: The drywall has crumbled here, exposing the brickwork.

Below: On the top floor of the building underneath one of the skylights.

Down in the basement of the building, you can see a mail chute on the right.

Inside of the many storage rooms in the basement.

6

EMERSON HIGH SCHOOL

Bearing the name of transcendentalist writer, lecturer, and philosopher, Ralph Waldo Emerson, Emerson School was Gary's first high school and was also the first public school in the city to implement Gary School Superintendent William Wirt's new Work-Study-Play system of education. Wirt developed a "Whole Child" philosophy while assuming the post of school superintendent in the city of Bluffton, Indiana, in 1899. He believed rapid urbanization occurring in the early twentieth century threatened the rural values necessary for the total development of a child, those values being family, work, and productivity. When Wirt became superintendent of schools of Gary in 1907, he began implementing his values into the school system by initiating teacher hiring standards, lengthening the school day, and designing schools to meet his standards.

Built in 1909, Ralph Waldo Emerson School was designed by St. Louis architect William Ittner and included no less than what Wirt required to implement his new system: thirty classrooms, seven laboratories, art studios, band, and orchestra rooms, and rooms for industrial and household arts. The school also boasted an auditorium, a gymnasium with an upstairs running track, the first high school to have an indoor swimming pool, and even a student-run bank and zoo.

Wirt's new system of education, dubbed the Gary Plan and often referred to as the "platoon system," called for students to be split into two platoons, the first utilizing the school's academic facilities while the second platoon utilized the non-academic facilities such as the gym and swimming pool. The constant movement and rotating of students would be efficient in keeping all facilities in use at all times, thus reducing cost. Under the new system, school officials could schedule a student twice as large as before into the same space by rotating students between specialized teachers who would teach a specific subject on a precise time schedule.

Emerson was originally an all-white school, but due to overcrowding in the 1920s, black students attended white schools for the first time. To alleviate overcrowding, Wirt approved the transfer of black students to Emerson; six black students attended Emerson in 1926 and another eighteen followed in 1927. The white community did not stand for it, with the white student body staging a walk-out which eventually culminated into a strike. Over 1,300 protestors, students, and parents stood outside Emerson refusing to go back inside or disperse until the black students were transferred out. Wirt made the decision to establish a new school for black students, Theodore Roosevelt High School, and transferred the students out of Emerson. The issue of desegregation returned in 1945 when hundreds of white students walked out of the newly integrated Froebel School, prompting a visit by Frank Sinatra to help ease tensions, speaking at the Gary Memorial Auditorium about equality and acceptance. In 1946, the Gary school board adopted a desegregation policy, but discrimination continued as Emerson's white student body staged a second walkout in protest. It wasn't until 1949 that Indiana state law desegregated public schools.

Due to a shrinking enrollment caused by the city's decline, Emerson closed as a high school in 1981 and reopened as a magnet school. The school was renovated in 1998, which included the addition of a computer lab and new stage drapery and rigging, and the indoor swimming pool was filled in and replaced with a shower and dressing room.

By 2007, Emerson had deteriorated to the point that it was negatively affecting the health of the students and it was soon discovered that mold was the culprit. Old plumbing had sprung leaks within the ceilings and walls of the school. In March 2008, a major clean-up effort was underway as drywall and ceiling tiles were replaced, leaky pipes were repaired, new carpeting was laid out, and the building received a new coat of paint. The following month, an early evaluation of the school's air quality brought positive news, and the school boards announced the cleanup was a success. A more-thorough evaluation was later conducted and found that not only the mold was still present, but it was much more severe than previously thought. With no funds left, the school board made the hard decision to close Emerson after serving the community for ninety-nine years.

The building was listed on the National Register of Historic Places in 1995, but despite its status and history, the building has sat vacant since its closure. The Emerson School made national headlines in 2015 when a seventeen-year-old girl was found strangled to death in the building, spotlighting the immense blight the city faces.

Right: The school was designed by St. Louis architect William Ittner.

Below: An extremely small classroom located on the backside of the school.

Above: A large room on the third floor of the building, although it's unknown what it was used for.

Left: Office desk for a Mr. Lemmon.

Lockers lined these hallways outside the school's administrative offices.

Looking towards the front entrance of the school with an emblem on the underside of the staircase with the letters "EHS."

Stairs leading up to the third floor of the building.

One of the first school auditoriums in Gary was this one in the former Emerson High School.

Crumbled drywall and ceiling tiles cover the floors of the second-floor halls.

One of the classrooms for music on the far right side of the building.

Left: A piano sits in front of a teacher's office.

Below: A small electric piano in one of the music classrooms.

Above: Destroyed and graffiti covered work stations in one of the many classrooms in the school.

Right: Decaying literature textbooks dating back to the mid-2000s.

7

HORACE MANN HIGH SCHOOL

Following the success of Gary School Superintendent William Wirt's new Work-Play-Study system of education at Emerson High School, Wirt drew up plans for the establishment of four schools over the next two decades. Froebel, Roosevelt, Lew Wallace, and Horace Mann were planned to be similar to Emerson, all three stories tall and constructed in the red brick with white trim classical composition style.

Bearing the name of Horace Mann, a politician known for his commitment to promoting public education, the school was the city's third high school when it opened in 1918 to serve the city's west side. When it first opened, the school consisted of two portable trailers, eventually expanding to five trailers the following year. Wirt realized that permanent structures were needed for the rapidly growing population in the city's west side, and so construction on the current Horace Mann School began in 1921. The east building was erected in 1922, and the west building followed in 1924 with the central building being completed on November 8, 1926. The central building boasted forty-eight classrooms, two libraries, an auditorium, a cafeteria, two gyms, and two swimming pools. While the central building served most of the school's functions, the west building initially served kindergarten through 3rd grade, but later expanded to include the music department, ROTC headquarters, additional classrooms and offices, and the school new gym which was added onto the rear of the building in 1985. The east building was mainly used for administration offices and the print department, which was located in the basement.

Wirt went a step further and brought in landscape architects who used dredging equipment to alter the property's topography, adding a lagoon and rolling hills. A rock garden was placed near the flag pole in front of the school, pedestrian bridges were constructed over the narrow portions of the pond, and a bird sanctuary was added. Essentially, Wirt had turned the school's front lawn into a public park. The grounds behind the school contained a gravel playground and athletic field surrounded by a running track.

The 1960s saw a lot of change not only in Horace Mann School, but Gary in general. Like Emerson, Horace Mann School was originally an all-white school, and just like Emerson, it was slow to desegregate, and it wasn't until the 1960s that Horace Mann finally integrated. Racial tensions were high in Gary as unemployment increased along with crime. Then in 1967, Gary elected Richard Gordon Hatcher as the city's first black mayor, marking the beginning of the "white flight" as thousands of white residents moved away from the city. Enrollment at Horace Mann had plummeted as did the city's population. Despite this, the school board was able to construct the aforementioned modern gym in the rear of the west building as well as a renovation to the cafeteria.

By 2002, schools in Gary were falling apart and the city hadn't constructed a new school in over thirty years. Running out of funds and options, the school board made the decision to restructure the school system starting by closing schools with low enrollment which included Horace Mann and on June 10, 2004, Horace Mann High School was closed down.

The welcoming sign outside the school building.

The front entrance of the school.

Staircases leading down to the school's entrance and up to the principal's office.

The school's auditorium was heavily damaged due to a fire in 2017.

Fire officials claim arson was the cause of the fire which destroyed the auditorium.

One of the many, many gyms in the schools.

A heavily graffitied hallway outside the gyms.

One half of a gym, which was separated by a large door.

School lockers line this hallway.

A graffiti covered classroom.

Stairs leading up to the principal's office.

One of the older gyms in the school.

Right: A spiral staircase leading up into the running track.

Below: The old gym with an indoor running track.

8

MAHENCHA APARTMENTS

Although it's referred to as the Mahencia Apartments by the city of Gary, the four-story Mahencha Apartments building was constructed in 1928 right across from Horace Mann High School. Built with red brick and stone trimmings, the U-shaped building featured a courtyard in the rear and was designed in a combination of architectural styles, most notably the Italianate style with its low-pitched roof, asymmetrical square tower, and the central stairway with an "eyebrow" above it.

The apartments were built mainly to house U.S. Steel management and city officials. One common tidbit that is usually tossed around is that former mayor A. Martin Katz once lived here. According to his son, Michael Katz, in an interview published in the September 29, 2013, issue of the *Post-Tribune*, his mother and father never lived there at all. In 1941, the newlywed couple put a deposit down and their lease application was accepted but they were told the next day the apartment was no longer available. Soon after, they saw an ad in the newspaper advertising apartments for rent at the Mahencha. They never received an explanation, but they knew it was because they were Jewish. A. Martin Katz would go on to serve as Gary city judge from 1955 to 1963, and mayor of Gary between 1963 and 1967. Katz lost the Democratic primary in 1967 to Richard G. Hatcher, who would be the city's mayor for the next twenty years and eventually own the Mahencha Apartments.

Richard Hatcher and his wife purchased the Mahencha Apartments in 1978 and renamed it the Hatcher Apartments, even though residents still referred to it as the Mahencha. The Hatchers ran the apartment building for just six years before shuttering it. In that time, the unattended structural issues had gotten worse, and Hatcher was either unwilling or financially unable to make any repairs. Residents reported water damage, mold issues, fixtures falling off the walls, and old wiring which caused infrequent blackouts. With these issues coupled with a lack of profitability, Hatcher made the decision to shut down operations in 1985. A former employee would later accuse the Hatchers of purposefully neglecting the property since they purchased it.

It was later reported that Richard Hatcher not paying property taxes on multiple properties he owned in Gary including two homes, several vacant lots, and of course the Mahencha. In March 1987, Hatcher acknowledged he had not paid taxes on the Mahencha in 1983, but this was due to an ongoing appeal with the city tax assessor, and that the unpaid taxes will be paid with the proceeds. He also added that he had been unsuccessful in selling the property. By 1988, the tax bill on the Mahencha Apartments was well over $38,500. The city of Gary would try to sell the property at the Lake County treasurer's tax auction but was unsuccessful. In 1989, the Hatchers filed an injunction to block the city from seizing the property, citing their ongoing appeal with the tax assessor. The Hatchers later filed a lawsuit against the Indiana State Board of Tax Commissioners over the appeal. As the Hatchers were still unable or unwilling to pay their taxes on the Mahencha, the city was adamant about seizing the property and selling it at the next county auction.

While these disputes were happening behind the scenes, the Mahencha sat abandoned where it became a new home for the homeless. Drug abuse and prostitution were recurring problems, along with theft and vandalism. Windows were smashed, piping and any other valuable metals were stripped from the building for salvage, and every fixture was removed. Gary's building code and enforcement department issued numerous $5,000 code violation fines which were unpaid and added to the Hatchers' growing bill to the city. The Hatchers initially tried fixing these issues by boarding up the building and sending out a crew to clean up the trash around the property, but a week later, the boards were pulled off, and trash littered the grounds once again. Eventually, the Hatchers stopped trying. By 1990, the Hatchers owed more than $56,000 in taxes and fines for the Mahencha. Despite the Hatchers' appeals and the lawsuit, the city seized the property in the early 1990s.

In the mid-1990s, the city of Gary donated the property to the Horace Mann-Ambridge Neighborhood Improvement Organization (HMANIO) with hopes that the non-profit organization would be able to renovate the building. Plans were drawn up to include nine one-bedroom units, twelve two-bedroom, and six three-bedroom units. HMANIO was expecting to receive tax credits and funding from the Redevelopment Commission through city-issued bonds. Unfortunately, the funding never came through and HMANIO's plan fell apart.

In 1999 the Redevelopment Commission approved the sale of the Mahencha to the Tree of Life Community Development Corporation. The Tree of Life announced in 2000 that they would be making repairs to the roof, but due to a lack of funding, that never happened. In April 2001, it was announced that they would be receiving $1 million from the city and would be using $500,000 of their own funds to renovate the building. That also never happened. That was the last attempt at renovating the building. On April 6, 2021, firefighters responded to a fire at the ninety-three-year-old derelict structure. When they arrived, the second and third floors were engulfed in flames. The building suffered excessive damage, leaving it entirely gutted.

Above: Different architectural features can be found on the building.

Right: The building featured brick and stone trimming and terracotta tiles.

Above: Looking out the front of the building, Horace Mann High can be seen in the distance.

Left: Black-and-white wallpaper depicting semi-nude women.

Above left: The one and only interior stairwell in the building.

Above right: Torn wallpaper adorns this wall in a former apartment unit.

Right: The remains of an old television set sits in an empty room.

Above: The corner apartment units were much larger than the others.

Left: Old wallpaper in what was the kitchen.

Above: Shiny, bright wallpaper lines these walls, reminiscent of Christmas wrapping paper.

Right: A fire destroyed one of the apartment units on the upper floors.

Above: A deflated sex doll can be found in the doorway on the ground.

Left: This room fared better than the adjacent fire ravaged rooms.

9

JEFFERSON ELEMENTARY SCHOOL

J efferson Elementary School opened its doors in 1971, bearing the name of the nation's third president. It was around this time that Gary's "white flight" was in full swing following years of racial tension and the voting in of Richard Gordon Hatcher, the city's first black mayor. The demographic in the city would change from a predominantly white population to black as many left Gary to the surrounding suburbs and cities.

As the city declined over the next few decades, so did the city's population, and in turn, enrollment at Gary's schools. Many parents opted to sending their children to charter and private schools due to the failures of the Gary Community School Corporation. It was estimated that for every child that leaves Gary's public school system, the district loses an estimated $8,000 in state funding. Many schools under their control had closed down due to a lack of funds to maintain them and consolidate the schools to cut costs. In 2017, Gary Community Corp became the first school system in Indiana involved in a state takeover. It was also the same year that the decision was made to close three more schools, Jefferson being one of them. After forty-six years, Jefferson closed its doors for the last time in June 2017. To cut further costs, the Gary Community Corp sold off many of their vacant schools, most of which had deteriorated beyond repair. Jefferson was sold to Indiana-American Water Co. for $150,000 and demolition of the school building began in July 2021.

The school gymnasium.

Fire damage can be seen in the corner of gym, likely caused by vandals.

Right: The school's mascots were the Jefferson Jaguars.

Below: School desks and workbooks lay scattered across this classroom.

Above: A mostly empty classroom.

Left: An American flag still hangs from a world map.

A classroom for teaching students math.

Boxes full of school workbooks and textbooks have sat here since the school's closure.

School desks and abandoned textbooks showcase how wasteful the Gary school district has been.

The school's library.

In comparison to other classrooms, this one is quite empty.

When the school closed, the cash starved school district left behind countless books, school desks, and other essentials.

It's assumed that all these school supplies were destroyed when the school building was demolished.

Most of the school's globes were found piled into this classroom.

10

AMERICAN STATE BANK

American State Bank was established in 1917 and the current bank building in Gary was constructed in 1924. Banking institutions in Lake County began to fail by the summer of 1930 towards the start of the Great Depression. In August of that year, the suicide of the president of the American State Bank of Gary started a series of withdrawals in banks throughout the region. The director of the American State Bank in Chicago disappeared after the bank abruptly shut down, only to be found a week later in Peoria, Illinois, supposedly suffering from amnesia. In September 1931, the president of Hammond's National Trust Bank was found guilty of illegal loans and overdrafts for which he was sentenced to prison. Then in 1932, the president of Indiana State Bank in Indiana Harbor was found guilty of embezzlement. Not long after, the president of Hammond's largest bank (the First Trust and Savings Bank) and his son, were convicted of making loans without the approval of the board of directors.

All of Hobart's banks closed by October 1931 and every bank in Hammond closed during 1932. By the end of 1932, thirty-three banks in Lake County had closed. Only three banks survived in East Chicago and only Gary National Bank survived in that city. Gary National Bank would acquire American State Bank and in 1983, they changed their name to Gainer Bank and later to NBD Bank in 1992, predecessors to Chase Bank. By 2000, the American State Bank building in Gary was no longer being used as a bank and was occupied by the city's Gary Probation Department, before the Indiana Department of Correction took over the responsibilities of the probation office. The bank has sat empty since at least 2015.

Above: The exterior features some Neo-Classical elements, which was common for banks of the time.

Left: A close-up of the bank vault.

Right: A wider view of the former bank lobby.

Below: Looking at the bank lobby from the second floor, one can see fire damage on the ceiling.

11

LOVELL'S BARBER COLLEGE

Lovell Amison was born in 1912 to Pearlene and Willie Amison in Tuscaloosa, Alabama. He came to Gary, Indiana, at an early age and it was there he met Zelda Laverne Perkins. The two married in 1953 and had one daughter together, Sheryl Denyce Amison, along with his stepson, Charles Banks, and two stepdaughters, Laverne Dillard and Charlene Fulton. Lovell opened the first Barber College in Northwest Indiana in 1959. He was well-liked and a well-known barber in the region, as well as a fierce boxing fan, and he loved going to boxing events. His wife died on March 23, 2002, and he soon followed on August 2, 2003. Their daughter, Sheryl, who worked at Lovell's Barber College for over twenty-three years, died in 2006.

The building located at 1700 Broadway was built in 1915 and was formerly known as Gary Federal Savings & Loan Association, located right next door to the former American State Bank, another banking institution. Lovell moved his college into the building when Gary Federal Savings merged with Citizens Financial Bank in 1983. Over the years, the lettering which read "GARY FEDERAL SAVINGS & LOAN ASSOCIATION" was removed for safety, and portions of the facade had fallen apart.

On October 9, 2020, contractors were working on the roof as the building was being converted into office space when a fire erupted, heavily damaging the second floor of the building. The owner, Vanessa Braxton, initially planned to open the building in March 2021 to include a medical office, a mobile phone store, fifteen office suites, a conference room, and a virtual office for small business owners. Despite the damages, Braxton said the basement and first floor were still usable and a new plan would be drawn up.

The building dates back to 1915 and was built for the Gary Federal Savings & Loan Association.

Towards Broadway on the ground floor of the former barber college.

A much wider view of the ground floor.

Looking towards the back of the building.

Right: Peeling paint and wallpaper in one of the back rooms.

Below: What was a small seating area.

12

NORTH GLEASON PARK PAVILION

Originating in 1920 as Riverside Park, North Gleason Park was just half of a 315-acre public park located on the Little Calumet River. The park was segregated into north and south sections divided by the river. South Gleason Park served the white residents of Gary and mainly consisted of an eighteen-hole golf course and a clubhouse designed by George Maher, while North Gleason Park served only black residents and featured athletic fields, tennis courts, an outdoor swimming pool, picnic pavilions, and an extremely popular nine-hole golf course which winded through the swamplands. North Gleason Park's funding would never equal that of South Gleason, and its location along the river's flood plain was less than ideal. Riverside Park was renamed after U.S. Steel superintendent and longtime park board president, William P. Gleason, in 1933.

During the Great Depression, the Works Progress Administration employed residents to help with construction and landscaping projects, providing daycare services and activities such as baseball, croquet, and checkers. The North Gleason Park Pavilion was constructed in 1941 and provided a large dance hall and assembly room, lunchroom, lounge, outdoor terrace, and locker rooms for golfers and swimmers. By the 1980s, the Pavilion housed the Gary Police Athletic League and a training center for boxers. Under the tutelage of a retired police officer and legendary boxing coach, John Taylor, countless fighters trained here like Light Welterweight World Champion "Merciless" Mary McGee and four-time world championship contender Angel "El Diablo" Manfredy, as well other professional boxers such as Orphius Waite, Jimmy Perez Jr., and Derrick Findley.

The building is in rough shape with mold, buckets catching water from the leaking roof, and fixtures that have been stolen by scrappers. The walls which were once shrines to boxing greats such as Muhammad Ali, Mike Tyson, and their own Angel Manfredy have been vandalized with posters and newspaper clippings ripped from the walls. In the past few years, local preservationists have attempted to preserve the building in a grassroots effort that involved cleaning up the property, boarding it up, and having it listed on the National Register of Historic Places.

Exterior of the North Gleason Park Pavilion.

A sign for the Police Athletic League established in 1985.

Rudy Clay served as mayor after Scott King, the last mayor to support the pavilion.

A steel plaque commemorating the opening of the pavilion.

The main lobby of the building.

Above: Various flyers, posters, and newspaper clipping adorned the walls dating back to the 1980s.

Left: A poster advertising a fight at the Reno Convention Center in Reno, NV.

Above: Some equipment was left behind when the gym closed down.

Right: A punching bag lays on the ground in front of posters and flyers dating back to the early 90s.

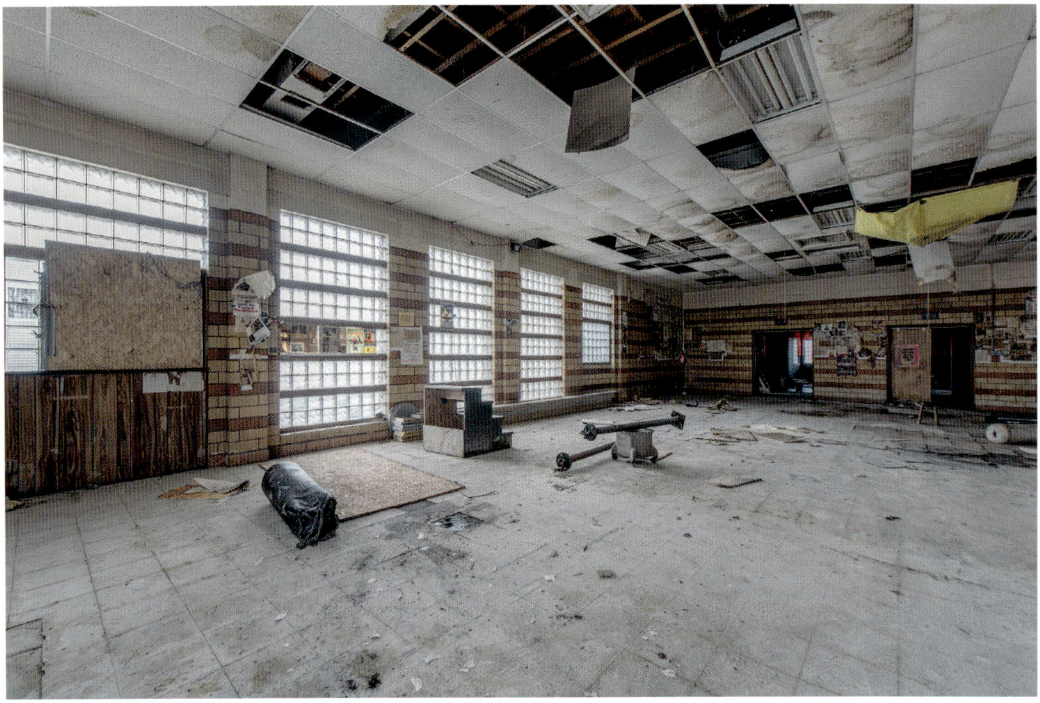

There was once a boxing ring in the middle of this room but was removed during a neighborhood cleanup of the building.

Above left: Old lockers with various flyers, newspaper clippings, and photos relating to boxing in Gary.

Above right: A newspaper clipping where Mary McGee from Gary won the fight against Kristy Follmar for the WBC International female lightweight title.

Above: Inside the coach's office.

Right: A flyer for a PAL fight taking place in Jacksonville, FL, in October 1987.

Above: Flyer for the PAL Boxing Championship, which took place in October 1989 in West Palm Beach, FL.

Left: More flyers and newspaper clipping related to the Gary PAL.

13

GARY SCREW & BOLT FACTORY

The Gary Screw & Bolt Company was founded in 1911 by a group of executives of the Pittsburgh Screw & Bolt Corporation and opened in the summer of 1912 with its first 100 employees. The company became an important defense contractor during World War II, employing 1,000 men and women, and manufacturing nearly 4,000 tons of bolts, nuts, rivets, threaded rods, and special fasteners monthly.

In 1947, a major fire destroyed two main buildings, reducing production by almost half. Despite that, the company retained over 900 employees and invested $1 million to expand and modernize the complex. The end came in the 1980s during a recession due to international competition resulting in the plant's closure on December 31, 1986, and all the equipment and machinery was sold to a liquidator.

The complex lay vacant until 2002 when it was purchased by the Gary Urban Enterprise Association (GUEA). The purpose was to use the building to store donated clothing before the clothing was cut up into strips and shipped to countries in need of bulk textiles. The city agreed to forgive all the back taxes on the property in exchange for the GUEA to conduct a basic environmental cleanup on the site and sell parcels back to the city upon request. It wasn't long before the organization was being investigated by the federal government.

Between 1998 and 2004, the executive director of the GUEA, Jojuana Lynn Meeks, purchased over 655 properties, and being a tax-exempt non-profit, the GUEA was required to submit a development plan to the Lake County Government showing its intent for these properties in order to maintain tax-free status. Meeks never reported these purchases. In addition, Meeks began transferring these properties to several companies she had created for a post-GUEA life. In 2006, Jojuana Lynn Meeks and Financial Manager Charmaine Pratchett were charged with misuse of public funds, under-reporting of funds, theft, excess pay, and malfeasance, among other criminal charges against them. Meeks received a six-year prison sentence, and Pratchett received a seven-year prison sentence. In addition to their convictions, Board members Derrick Earls and Johnnie Wright, Gregory Hill, Lawrence Meeks, Roosevelt Powell, Willie Harris, and Will Smith were convicted of corruption, fraud, theft, and wrongdoing.

Once again, the former Gary Screw & Bolt Company factory laid vacant and remains so to this day. A rather controversial thing was left behind: hundreds of pounds of clothing donated to the GUEA, now decaying on the factory floor. Environmental Cleansing Corporation, a demolition and recycling firm, bought the property in 2014 to store scrap metal, wood, concrete, glass, and paper with some of the scrap being sold to nearby steel mills. The company planned on maintaining their headquarters here and building a rail spur to connect to the Norfolk and Southern rail line on Screw & Bolt's south side. A portion of the factory was also planned to be demolished, which eventually occurred in September 2021.

Inside one of the massive factory buildings on the property.

The factory shutdown in 1987 and hasn't been used as a factory since.

Left: A massive area leading outside, although I'm uncertain if there was machinery here at one point or if this was used for semi-trucks.

Right: Thousands of pounds of old clothing sit in one of the old factory buildings.

Below: The clothing here was donated, a reminder of a corrupt scheme by the organization's executive director.

Wash basins for workers of the factory.

Several wash basins in what was a shower and washroom area for workers.